POC
Cr

POCKET GUIDE TO CROCHET

Landauer Publishing, www.landauerpub.com, is an imprint of
Fox Chapel Publishing Company, Inc.

Project Team
Managing Editor: Gretchen Bacon
Acquisitions Editor: Amelia Johanson
Editor: Sherry Vitolo
Designer: Mike Deppen

ISBN 978-1-63981-072-7

Library of Congress Control Number: 2024931100
We are always looking for talented authors. To submit an idea,
please send a brief inquiry to acquisitions@foxchapelpublishing.com.

Printed in China

First printing

POCKET GUIDE TO
Crochet

Take-Along Information on Tools, Popular Stitches, Tips, and Tricks

Jen Lucas

Contents

Introduction

Whether you are new to crocheting or have been stitching for decades, there are always those little things that you need to look up. Maybe you forgot how to start a project with foundation single crochet (this is the one I always have to look up) or you're looking for a simple stitch pattern for a baby blanket. This pocket guide is meant to give you a quick reference for all the traditional crochet basics.

We'll start with a review of all the materials you'll need to get started on any crochet project. Then we'll move to important topics like abbreviations and gauge. With that pesky gauge discussion out of the way, we can move on to the more fun fundamentals—the stitches! You'll find clear step-by-step photos for how to create the most common stitches in crochet.

I'll share with you some of the most classic and commonly used stitch patterns, such as moss stitch, blanket stitch, and granny squares. This little book is packed with the crochet information you've always wanted to keep in your back pocket—and now can. Let's get stitching!

—Jen *(she/her)*

Crochet hooks are available in a variety of styles and sizes and are made from a variety of materials.

Crochet Hooks

With so many different types of traditional crochet hooks on the market, how do you know which one is right for you? Like many things in this craft, it often comes down to personal preference as well as the project you're working on. There are so many details to consider—some hooks have pointier tips, some have ergonomic handles, etc. Experiment with different types of hooks to find the styles you like best.

Aluminum hooks—These hooks are among the most common you'll see crocheters using for their projects. The aluminum crochet hook is both lightweight and durable, as well as very affordable. These hooks allow the yarn to glide easily as you work, making them a great choice for most projects.

Plastic or acrylic hooks—Plastic and acrylic hooks are also fairly common and inexpensive, and they come in a variety of fun colors. The yarn will easily slide on the surface, much like an aluminum hook.

Wooden hooks—You'll find wooden crochet hooks made from all sorts of wood. While the crochet hook feels smooth, it often has a bit of a "grip" to it from the wood grain. This makes these hooks a good choice for yarns that can be slippery, such as bamboo or silk.

Ergonomic hooks—Many crochet hooks of all materials now come with ergonomic handles on them. Having a hook with a larger and more comfortable handle is great for those long crochet sessions, when you just can't seem to put your project down. You can find both handmade and commercially made ergonomic hooks.

CROCHET HOOK GUIDE

US Size	Millimeters
B-1	2.25mm
C-2	2.75mm
D-3	3.25mm
E-4	3.5mm
F-5	3.75mm
G-6	4.0mm
7	4.5mm
H-8	5.0mm
I-9	5.5mm
J-10	6.0mm
K-10½	6.5mm
L-11	8.0mm
M/N-13	9.0mm
N/P-15	10.0mm
P-16	11.5mm
P/Q	15.0mm
Q	15.75mm

Yarn is available in a kaleidoscope of colors, from solid shades to mottled rainbows.

Yarns

Besides the crochet hook, the other material you absolutely need for your crochet project is the yarn. The possibilities are seemingly endless when it comes to yarn. Yarn choice significantly affects the texture, drape, and overall aesthetic of the finished piece, so take time figuring out what you like best and what will work for your project.

You might find that for projects like shawls and sweaters, you want to use a hand-dyed, luxurious yarn; however, for projects like baby hats and blankets, a less expensive, commercially available yarn may be the right option. Much like crochet hooks, yarn is also a personal choice. You might find that you love working with wool, or maybe you're like me and you love crocheting with cotton yarn. Spend some time thinking about the project and how it will be used—that will help guide your decision toward the best fiber for the project.

The yarn's weight, thickness, and texture will determine the weight, thickness, and texture of your final piece.

One of the critical factors to consider when choosing yarn is the thickness. Yarn thickness is defined by the yarn weight, and there are industry standards that almost every yarn company uses. If you find a pattern that calls for a "#4/Worsted/Medium yarn," that is the yarn weight you'll want to use for your project. Changing the weight of the yarn you're using for a pattern greatly affects the gauge of the project. Some crocheters may be comfortable with changing the weight of the yarn for a specific pattern, which is amazing; just know that most of the time, this change comes with some calculating you will have to do on your own.

1, Fingering

4, Worsted

4, Heavy Worsted

5, Bulky

The difference in yarn weights can be subtle, but it's very noticeable when you compare a few strands in different sizes.

Yarns Used

For the examples in this book, I used the following yarns:

- **Herrschners Worsted Yarn:** *herrschners.com*
  - ›› *Used for Moss Stitch (p.60), Blanket Stitch (p.61), and Granny Stripe (p.62).*
- **Lion Brand® Pima Cotton Yarn:** *lionbrand.com*
  - ›› *Used for Sophie Baby Blanket Pattern on page 69.*
- **Red Heart Super Saver Yarn:** *yarnspirations.com*
  - ›› *Used for other example yarn photos.*
- **WeCrochet Wool of the Andes Worsted and Swish Worsted:** *crochet.com*
  - ›› *Used for Granny Square (p.63).*

YARN WEIGHT GUIDE

Here's a quick reference of the Standard Yarn Weight System from the Craft Yarn Council. Remember, this chart is just a guide—it's a starting point. If you're working from a specific pattern, follow the yarn weight and gauge information for that project.

YARN WEIGHT GUIDE			
Yarn Weight & Name	**Type of Yarn**	**Gauge in Single Crochet over 4"**	**Recommended US Hook Size**
LACE 0	Lace, 10-count crochet thread	N/A*	N/A*
SUPER FINE 1	Sock, Fingering, Baby	21–32 sts	B-1–E-4
FINE 2	Sport, Baby	16–20 sts	E-4–7
LIGHT 3	DK, Light Worsted	12–17 sts	7–I-9
MEDIUM 4	Worsted, Heavy Worsted, Afghan, Aran	11–14 sts	I-9–K-10½
BULKY 5	Bulky, Chunky	8–11 sts	K-10½–M/N-13
SUPER BULKY 6	Super Bulky, Craft	7–9 sts	M/N-13–Q
JUMBO 7	Jumbo, Roving	6 sts or less	Q and larger

*Lace yarns are typically crocheted using larger hooks to create loose, lacy patterns.
Be sure to follow the recommendations for hook size and gauge included in your pattern.

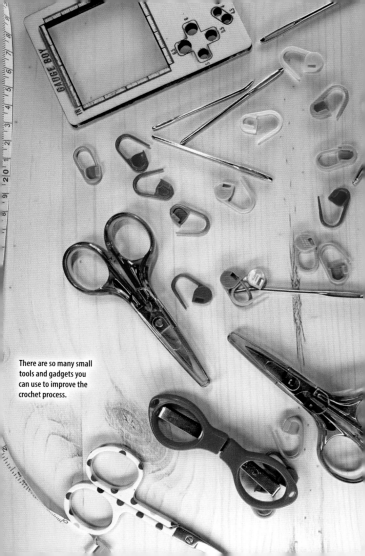

There are so many small tools and gadgets you can use to improve the crochet process.

Notions

What are notions? They are all the little tools you might need to complete your project. This includes tools like stitch markers, scissors, tapestry needles, and more!

Stitch markers—Stitch markers are used in projects for a variety of reasons. They come in many different types and colors, so you can use different ones to keep things organized as you work. You may need to mark a specific stitch (like in the Sophie Baby Blanket Pattern on page 69), or simply need to mark the Right Side or Wrong Side of your project, if there is a designation in the pattern. A locking stitch marker is a great tool to have when you set down your project for a while—use it to hold onto the working loop of your project so that it doesn't come unraveled.

Use stitch markers to keep track of stitches or to note the Right Side or Wrong Side of a piece.

Scissors—When your crochet project is complete, you'll need to cut the yarn with scissors to leave a yarn tail to weave in. There are so many different types of scissors and cutting tools you can use. I personally love little folding travel scissors. They are lightweight and small enough that you can easily toss them into your project bag.

Tapestry needles— Tapestry needles (also known as yarn needles or darning needles) are a necessary notion for completing your project. While these needles are often simply used to weave in the ends, you can also use them for things like adding embroidery to a piece.

When choosing a tapestry needle, make sure the eye of the needle isn't too big. You want to make sure the needle can work in and out of your stitches smoothly, and you don't want the eye to be so large that it starts to stretch your stitches. Many tapestry needles are sold in packs, and often one pack will contain a variety of sizes.

Measuring tools—Many different measuring tools serve many different purposes in crochet. You can use a tape measure for checking gauge and the measurements of your project as you go. Gauge rulers are also great for checking gauge, and often come with holes for checking crochet hook and knitting needle sizes. Like everything that comes along with this hobby, you can purchase measuring tools at a big-box store or find special handmade measuring notions at local yarn shops and yarn festivals.

With just a hook, some yarn, and the following techniques, you can make an assortment of crocheted fabrics.

Crochet Basics

With our tools ready, let's start on the crochet basics. All it takes is knowledge of a few stitches to create just about any motif you can think of. Once you learn the fundamentals like chain, slip stitch, single crochet, double crochet, and treble crochet, you can build on them to create more complex patterns.

READING A PATTERN

After choosing a pattern, it's important to read through the whole thing before getting started. You can be as quick or as thorough as you like with this step. I've found that taking just five to ten minutes to read through the pattern saves me a lot of time later. I can take note of anything that seems confusing to look up later in my *Pocket Guide to Crochet* or online. I also use this time to highlight or mark any sizing information in the pattern as well.

It's also important to note the terminology used in the pattern. You'll commonly find patterns written either in US terms or in UK terms, and it's critical to know which one your pattern is using. Each of these terminologies uses similar words, but these words may describe different actions. For example, a single crochet in US terms is called a double crochet in UK terms. This book is written in US terms.

Here's a quick reference guide for converting the most common US terms to UK terms (and vice versa):

US/UK TERMS	
US Terms	**UK Terms**
Slip Stitch (sl st)	Slip Stitch (ss)
Single Crochet (sc)	Double Crochet (dc)
Half Double Crochet (hdc)	Half Treble Crochet (htr)
Double Crochet (dc)	Treble Crochet (tr)
Treble Crochet (tr)	Double Treble Crochet (dtr)

ABBREVIATIONS

Crochet patterns typically use abbreviations in the instructions. While it might seem a little confusing at first, it makes the pattern much easier to read and understand. Here are some of the most common abbreviations. I use them throughout this book.

beg	begin(ning)	**sc**	single crochet
BLO	back loop only	**sl st**	slip stitch
bp	back post	**sp(s)**	space(s)
ch(s)	chain(s)	**st(s)**	stitch(es)
dc	double crochet	**t-ch**	turning chain
FLO	front loop only	**tr**	treble crochet
fp	front post	**WS**	Wrong Side
hdc	half double crochet	**yo**	yarn over
inv dec	invisible decrease	*****	repeat directions given from *
rep	repeat		
rnd(s)	round(s)	**( ) or [ ]**	work stitches within ( ) or [ ] as many times as specified by the number immediately following
RS	Right Side		

GAUGE

Gauge is such an important part of a crochet project. This measurement, also sometimes referred to as tension, is simply the number of stitches and rows (or rounds) in a specified area (length and width). This is often written over 2" (5.1cm) square or 4" (10.2cm) square. To measure the gauge, you lay a tape measure or other measuring tool on top of your piece and count the number of stitches and rows in the area.

There are 17 stitches in the 4" (10.2cm) section of this row.

The gauge is measured, so now what? You'll need to compare your gauge with the gauge listed in the pattern. If you have too many stitches, go up a hook size or two. If you have too few stitches, use a smaller-sized hook to make the stitches a little bit smaller. Remember—every crocheter tensions their yarn in different ways. The hook sizes listed on the ball band on a skein of yarn or in a pattern are simply a jumping-off point!

These three swatches have the same number of single crochet stitches, but I used different hook sizes for each—making a noticeable difference in the finished swatch size.

Another point about gauge is that it will affect the amount of yarn you need to complete a project. This becomes tricky for projects like blankets and scarves (or other projects that don't need to fit a body). I know most of us feel the urge to skip the gauge swatch step because we think the size of the finished object isn't super important. While that may be true, a gauge that is wildly off from the pattern can have a great effect on the amount of yarn used. No one wants to run out of gradient yarn two-thirds of the way through their blanket project!

SLIP KNOT

A slip knot is the first step to starting most crochet projects. It's created and the loop is placed on the hook. From that single loop, the rest of the stitches are worked. These are typically chain stitches, which become the foundation chain. There are lots of ways to make a slip knot—this is the method I like to use when teaching others about the crochet basics. It's both easy to do and easy to learn.

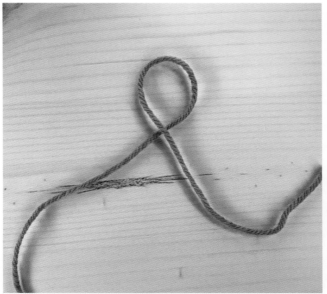

1. Leaving a 4"–6" (10.2–15.2cm) yarn tail, create a loop. The yarn tail should go over the working yarn (the yarn coming from the ball or skein).

2. Fold the loop down over the working yarn. You should have something that looks a bit like a pretzel.

3. You'll see three strands, with the center strand being the working yarn. Place your crochet hook through the loop, going over the bottom strand, under the middle strand, and over the top strand as shown.

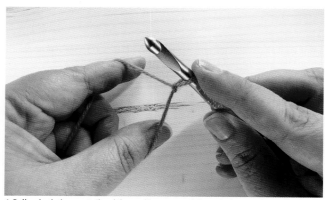

4. Pull on both the yarn tail and the working yarn to tighten the loop on the crochet hook. Your slip knot is complete.

FOUNDATION CHAIN

For the foundation chain, chain stitches are created off the initial slip knot. The next row or round of stitches will then be worked into this foundation chain. You'll sometimes see this called the starting chain.

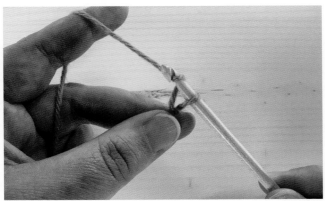

1. With the slip knot on the crochet hook, bring the working yarn over the hook from the back of the hook to the front as shown (this is a yarn over).

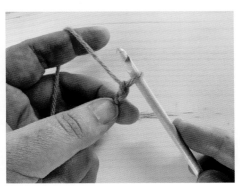

2. Use the hook to draw the yarn back through the first loop (the slip knot) on the hook to create a chain stitch.

3. Yarn over.

4. Draw the yarn through the loop on the hook to create another chain stitch.

5. Repeat steps 3 and 4 until you've created the desired number of chain stitches.

WORKING INTO THE CHAIN

Once the foundation chain (or starting chain) is created, it's time to work into that chain to start creating your crocheted fabric. Like many things in crochet, how you work into the chain is often based on personal preference. Be sure to check your pattern for instructions on how to work into the chain—sometimes the chain will be worked into again later in the pattern, so how you work into the chain from the start will be important.

There are three strands that make up the chain—two strands on the front that form a braid and look like little V shapes and a third strand on the back side, which is referred to as the back or "back bumps" of the chain.

The front side of the foundation chain has two strands that form V shapes.

The back side of the foundation chain has one strand that rises up in small bumps.

If the pattern doesn't specify how to work into the foundation chain, I prefer to work into the back of the chain. I like this method because it allows the front of the chain (the part that looks like a braid) to run along the bottom of the fabric, making for a nice edging.

You can work a variety of stitches into the foundation chain, and your pattern will tell you exactly what stitches to use.

Working into the bumps on the back side of the foundation chain will create a neat edge, but your pattern may require something different, so be certain to check first.

SLIP STITCH

This is the shortest stitch in crochet. It is typically used for projects where you want to create a dense fabric. You'll see it used in home items and some variations are used to add details on accessories and garments.

To work a slip stitch, follow these steps:

1. Insert the hook into the desired stitch.

2. Yarn over.

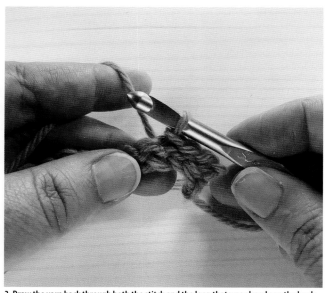

3. Draw the yarn back through both the stitch and the loop that was already on the hook. The slip stitch is complete.

Fabric Pattern:

To work a fabric made of slip stitches in rows, ch any number of sts to create the foundation chain.

Row 1 (RS): Sl st in each ch across, turn.

Row 2: Sl st in each st across, turn.

Rep Row 2 for pattern.

Single crochet stitches are taller than slip stitches, but still create a dense fabric.

SINGLE CROCHET

The single crochet stitch is slightly taller than the slip stitch. It's one of the most common stitches you'll find in crochet. You can make just about anything using only single crochet stitches, but it is an especially useful stitch for projects like amigurumi figures and baby items.

To make a single crochet stitch, follow these steps:

1. Insert the hook into the desired stitch.

2. Yarn over.

3. Draw the yarn back through the stitch. You should have two loops on the hook.

4. Yarn over.

5. Draw the yarn back through the two loops to complete the stitch. Repeat these steps, working into the next stitch across the row.

Fabric Pattern:

To work a fabric made of single crochet stitches in rows, ch any number of sts to create the foundation chain.

Row 1 (RS): Beg with the second ch from the hook, sc into each ch across, ch 1 (does not count as a st), turn.

Row 2: Sc in each st across, ch 1, turn.

Rep Row 2 for pattern.

Half double crochet stitches are taller and create a more flexible fabric.

HALF DOUBLE CROCHET

Fabric made with half double crochet is extra squishy due to the construction of the stitch. It's quick and easy, making it perfect for baby items like blankets and bibs.

To make a half double crochet stitch, follow these steps:

1. Yarn over.

2. Insert the hook into the desired stitch.

3. Yarn over.

4. Draw the yarn back through the stitch. You should have three loops on the hook.

5. Yarn over.

6. Draw the yarn back through all three loops to complete the stitch. Repeat these steps, working into the next stitch across the row.

Fabric Pattern:

To work a fabric made of half double crochet stitches in rows, ch any number of sts to create the foundation chain.

Row 1 (RS): Beg with the third ch from hook, hdc into each ch across, ch 2 (counts as hdc), turn.

Row 2: Hdc in each st across, ch 2 (counts as hdc), turn.

Rep Row 2 for pattern.

Double crochet stitches are common tall stitches you can use to quickly work up a piece.

DOUBLE CROCHET

Double crochet is the most versatile of all the basic crochet stitches. It's used most often, and you can create all sorts of interesting motifs building off this stitch.

To make the double crochet stitch, follow these steps:

1. Yarn over.

2. Insert the hook into the desired stitch.

3. Yarn over.

4. Draw the yarn back through the stitch. You should have three loops on the hook.

5. Yarn over.

6. Draw the yarn back through the first two loops on the hook. You should have two loops on the hook.

7. Yarn over. Draw the yarn back through the last two loops, completing the stitch.

Fabric Pattern:

To work a fabric made of double crochet stitches in rows, ch any number of sts to create the foundation chain.

Row 1 (RS): Beg with the fourth ch from hook, dc into each ch across, ch 3 (counts as dc), turn.

Row 2: Dc in each st across, ch 3 (counts as dc), turn.

Rep Row 2 for pattern.

Treble crochet creates an airy, very flexible fabric.

TREBLE CROCHET

Treble crochet, also sometimes called triple crochet, is a stitch even taller than the double crochet. Because of its height, it makes a surprisingly lacy and airy stitch.

To make the treble crochet stitch, follow these steps:

1. Yarn over twice, bringing the yarn from the back of the hook to the front of the hook.

2. Insert the hook into the desired stitch.

3. Yarn over, bringing the yarn from the back of the hook to the front of the hook.

4. Draw the yarn back through the stitch. You should have four loops on the hook.

5. Yarn over. Draw the yarn back through the first two loops. You should have three loops on the hook.

6. Yarn over. Draw the yarn back through the first two loops. You should have two loops on the hook.

7. Yarn over. Draw the yarn back through the last two loops, completing the stitch. Repeat these steps, working into the stitch across the row.

Fabric Pattern:

To work a fabric made of treble crochet stitches in rows, ch any number of sts to create the foundation chain.

Row 1 (RS): Beg with the fifth ch from hook, tr into each ch across, ch 4 (counts as tr), turn.

Row 2: Tr in each st across, ch 4 (counts as tr), turn.

Rep Row 2 for pattern.

FRONT LOOP ONLY/BACK LOOP ONLY

Most commonly, you'll work into the top of the stitch under both loops.

Patterns will sometimes tell you to work into the front loop only (often abbreviated as FLO) or into the back loop only (often abbreviated as BLO). Working into the front loop or back loop only gives a different look to the fabric, often adding an interesting texture. You can use this in lots of applications in your crochet—I especially love creating ribbing in my projects by working into the back loop only.

To work into the front loop only, insert the hook under only the front loop of the top of the stitch.

To work into the back loop only, insert the hook under only the back loop of the top of the stitch.

FRONT POST/BACK POST

To work a front post stitch, work your hook around the stitch's post from the front of the fabric. Your hook moves from the front of the fabric to the back to the front.

Not only can you work into the top of a crochet stitch, but you can also work around the post of the stitch. This provides a great deal of texture to a stitch pattern, and you'll often see it used in double crochet to create crocheted cables.

To work a back post stitch, work your hook around the stitch's post from the back of the fabric. Your hook moves from the back of the fabric to the front to the back.

FOUNDATION SINGLE CROCHET

The foundation single crochet is a very useful technique, especially for patterns where you need to create a long starting chain, like for an afghan, and the first row calls to work single crochets into that chain. With foundation single crochet, you create both the foundation chain and the first row of single crochet at the same time.

1. Starting with a slip knot on the hook, chain two.

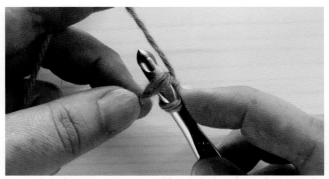

2. Insert the hook into the second chain stitch from the hook, working under two strands of the chain.

3. Yarn over. Draw the yarn back through one loop. You should have two loops on the hook.

4. Yarn over. Draw the yarn back through only the first loop. You should have two loops on the hook. This creates the next chain stitch of the starting chain.

It can be helpful to add a removeable stitch marker to this next chain stitch.

5. Yarn over. Draw the yarn back through both loops to complete the single crochet. You should have one loop on the hook.

6. Insert the hook under the two strands of the next chain stitch created in step 4.

7. Repeat steps 4 through 6 to create as many stitches as desired. End the row with step 5 to complete your foundation single crochet.

WHETHER TO COUNT TURNING CHAINS

In a pattern, sometimes the turning chain counts as a stitch and sometimes it does not. For single crochet, unless otherwise specified, the "ch 1" does not count as a stitch. For other stitches, the pattern will tell you whether it counts as a stitch. Let's look at an example in double crochet.

If a pattern says the beginning chain **does not** count as a stitch, you'll work a double crochet into the first stitch from the previous row.

If a pattern tells you that the beginning chain **does** count as stitch, you'll skip that first stitch (because your chain is the stitch), and you'll work your stitch into the next stitch of the previous row.

MAGIC RING

The magic ring, also known as the adjustable loop or sliding loop, is the perfect start to a project worked in the round from the center out. Several stitches can be worked into the ring (or loop), creating a center with no hole in it. This technique is perfect for projects like top-down hats and amigurumi figures.

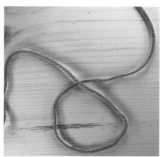

1. Leaving a 4"–6" (10.2–15.2cm) yarn tail, create a loop. The yarn tail should go under the working yarn.

2. Pick up the ring, pinching the point where the yarn crosses over itself.

3. Insert the hook into the center of ring. Catch the working yarn and draw it back through the ring as shown.

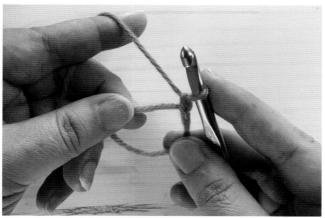

4. Create the number of chain stitches needed for the stitch you are working with (see the chart on page 54). For single crochet, you need to make one chain.

5. Work the number of stitches needed into the ring, working over both the ring and the yarn tail. For single crochet, you need to work six stitches into the ring.

6. Once all the stitches are worked, pull on the yarn tail to close the ring. You're ready to work in the round.

The pattern you are using will tell you exactly how many of the specific stitches need to be worked into the ring. If a simple circle is being worked, there is a general rule for how many stitches to work into the ring. This can vary slightly depending on your yarn type and gauge, especially as the stitches get taller, but use this chart as a starting point for any projects that require a circle made with a magic ring:

MAGIC RING		
Stitch	**Instructions**	**Total Sts**
Single Crochet	Ch 1 (does not count as st), 6 sc into ring	6
Half Double Crochet	Ch 2 (counts as st), 8 hdc into ring	9
Double Crochet	Ch 3 (counts as st), 11 dc into ring	12
Treble Crochet	Ch 4 (counts as st), 17 tr into ring	18

INCREASING & DECREASING

Increasing in crochet can be done in a variety of ways. The easiest way to increase is to simply work more than one stitch into the stitch from the previous row. For example, a pattern may call for "2 dc into next st" as an increase.

Work two stitches into a single stitch from the previous row to add width to a project.

Simple decreases in crochet are almost as easy as increases! To decrease two stitches together, work the first stitch up until the final step (when you have two loops on the hook). Do not complete the stitch, instead work another stitch in the next stitch up to the final step (when you have three loops on the hook). Yarn over and draw the yarn back through all three loops to create a single decrease.

Here's an example using double crochet:

1. Work double crochet up to the final step. You should have two loops on the hook.

2. Work another double crochet into the next stitch up to the final step. You should have three loops on the hook.

3. Yarn over and draw the yarn back through all three loops to complete the decrease.

Invisible Decrease

The invisible decrease, often abbreviated as inv dec, is a decrease commonly used in amigurumi projects worked in single crochet. It creates a decrease that blends into the fabric well, hence the name. Some patterns call for this decrease to be completed by working under the front loop of both stitches in the decrease; however, I prefer to work under the front loop only of the first stitch, then under both loops of the second stitch as I think it creates the most invisible single crochet decrease.

1. Insert the hook under the front loop of the next stitch.

2. Insert the hook under both loops of the next stitch.

3. Yarn over and draw the yarn back through the loops from steps 1 and 2. You should have two loops on the hook.

4. Yarn over and draw the yarn back through the two loops on the hook, completing the decrease.

FINISHING: FASTEN OFF & WEAVE IN ENDS

Once a project is complete, it's time to do the odds and ends that make the project truly shine. Finishing your project can involve a lot of different techniques, but most commonly you'll need to fasten off the project and weave in all the ends.

With the project fastened off, it's time to weave in any remaining yarn tails. If there is an obvious Wrong Side to the piece, weave the ends in on the Wrong Side of the fabric. Use a tapestry needle to work the tail in and out of the stitches. Make sure the tapestry needle has an appropriately sized eye and take care not to pull on the tail too much while weaving in—you don't want to distort the fabric! Trim any remaining yarn tail.

To fasten off, simply trim the working yarn with scissors, leaving a tail that is about 6"–8" (15.2–20.3cm) long. Bring the tail of the yarn through the final working loop.

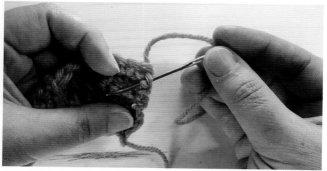

Use a light touch when weaving in ends to avoid distorting the fabric.

Stitch Patterns

The following are a few of the most beloved crochet stitch patterns. You can use these alone or in combination to create unique pieces.

MOSS STITCH

The moss stitch creates a dense, soft fabric.

Ch an odd number of chs.

Row 1 (RS): Beg in second ch from hook, sc into each ch across, ch 1 (does not count as st), turn.

Row 2 (WS): Sc in first st, *ch 1, skip next st, sc in next st; rep from * across, ch 1, turn.

Row 3: Sc in first sc, *sc in ch-sp, ch 1, skip next sc; rep from * across to last ch-sp, sc in ch-sp, sc in last sc, ch 1, turn.

Row 4: Sc in first sc, *ch 1, skip next sc, sc in ch-sp; rep from * across to last sc, sc in last sc, ch 1, turn.

Rep Rows 3 and 4 for pattern.

BLANKET STITCH

The blanket stitch creates a thick, warm texture and works up quickly.

Ch a multiple of 3 chs.

Row 1: 2 dc in third ch from hook, *skip next 2 chs, (sc, 2 dc) in next ch; rep from * across to last 3 chs, skip 2 chs, sc in last ch, ch 2 (does not count as st), turn.

Row 2: 2 dc in first sc, *skip next 2 dc, (sc, 2 dc) in next sc; rep from * across to last sc, sc in last sc, ch 2, turn.

Rep Row 2 for pattern.

GRANNY STRIPE

The granny stripe pattern creates an open, airy fabric.

Ch a multiple of 3 plus 1 chs.

Row 1 (RS): Dc in fourth ch from hook, *skip next 2 chs, 3 dc in next ch; rep from * across to last 3 chs, skip next 2 chs, 2 dc in last ch, ch 3 (counts as dc), turn.

Row 2 (WS): *3 dc in sp between two 3-dc-groups from row below; rep from * across, dc in top of beg-ch-3, ch 3 (counts as dc), turn.

Row 3: Dc in first st, *3 dc in sp between next two 3-dc-groups from row below; rep from * across, 2 dc in top of beg-ch-3, ch 3 (counts as dc), turn.

Rep Rows 2 and 3 for pattern.

Tip: You can create stripes by changing colors every row or two (or three or more—it's up to you!). To change colors, work the final stitch of the row before you want to change colors up to the final step (when two loops remain on your hook). Drop the old color and complete the stitch with the new color, then continue working in the pattern.

GRANNY SQUARE

The classic granny square is versatile and can be used as a building block for many types of crochet pieces.

Ch 6. Sl st into first ch to form ring.

Rnd 1: Ch 3 (counts as dc here and throughout), 2 dc in ring, (ch 3, 3 dc in ring) 3 times, ch 1, hdc in top of beg-ch-3, do not turn, continue working in joined rnds.

Rnd 2: Ch 3, 2 dc around post of hdc, [ch 1, (3 dc, ch 3, 3 dc) in ch-3 sp] 3 times, ch 1, 3 dc in next ch-3 sp, ch 1, hdc in top of beg-ch-3, do not turn.

Rnd 3: Ch 3, 2 dc around post of hdc, [ch 1, 3 dc in ch-1 sp, ch 1, (3 dc, ch 3, 3 dc) in ch-3 sp] 3 times, ch 1, 3 dc in ch-1 sp, 3 dc in ch-3 sp, ch 1, hdc in top of beg-ch-3, do not turn.

Rnd 4: Ch 3, 2 dc around post of hdc, [(ch 1, 3 dc in ch-1 sp) to ch-3 sp, ch 1, (3 dc, ch 3, 3 dc) in ch-3 sp] 3 times, (ch 1, 3 dc in ch-1 sp) to last ch-3 sp, ch 1, 3 dc in ch-3 sp, ch1, hdc in top of be- ch-3, do not turn.

Fasten off or continue working Rnd 4 to desired size.

SINGLE CROCHET BORDER

Making three single crochet stitches into the corner of your piece will ensure a clean, flat finish.

A single crochet border is a great way to finish many projects. It makes the sides of your project nice and even, giving them a clean and polished look. When working a single crochet border on a piece, be sure to add three single crochet stitches (3 sc) into the corner, so the corner will lay flat.

If the edges of your piece seem to ruffle, you may have made too many stitches in your border. If they are curling, you may have made too few.

When working along the side edges of your piece, take care to work the stitches evenly down the side. If your edge starts to ruffle, you may have too many stitches in your single crochet border. If the edge starts to curl in on itself, you may need to add additional stitches.

CRAB STITCH

The crab stitch, also known as reverse single crochet, creates a corded decorative edging to your piece. First, with the RS facing you (RS-facing), work a single crochet border around the entire edge. Do not turn, and work the crab stitch as follows:

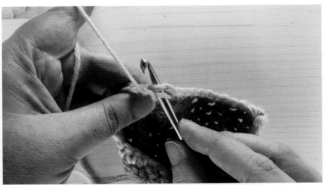

1. With RS-facing, insert the hook back into the stitch to the right of the working loop.

2. Yarn over and draw the yarn back through one loop. You should have two loops on the hook.

3. Yarn over and draw the yarn back through the two loops to complete the stitch. You should have one working loop on the hook.

4. Repeat steps 1 through 3 around the entire edge. When you get back to the beginning, fasten off and weave in the ends.

The finished blanket is lightweight but still sturdy and kid-friendly!

Sophie Baby Blanket Pattern

This is the perfect car seat–sized blanket that can easily be enlarged by adding more yarn! I've included the gauge and estimated finished size below. Gauge is not critical for this pattern; however, a different gauge will affect the amount of yarn needed as well as the finished size of the blanket.

Finished Size: 36" x 32" (91.4 x 81.3cm)

Gauge: 12 sts x 11 rows = 4" (10.2cm) square in pattern

TOOLS AND MATERIALS

- 500 yds. (457.2m) worsted weight (Medium #4) yarn in Color A
  - *I used 3 balls of Lion Brand Pima Cotton Yarn in Mineral Yellow*
- 550 yds. (502.9m) worsted weight (Medium #4) yarn in Color B
  - *I used 3 balls of Lion Brand Pima Cotton Yarn in Dragonfly*
- US H-8 (5.0mm) crochet hook, or size needed to obtain gauge
- 4 locking stitch markers
- Tapestry needles

To change colors, work the final stitch of the row before you want to change colors up to the final step (when two loops remain on your hook). Drop the old color and complete the stitch with the new color, then continue working in the pattern.

Main Body of Blanket

With Color A, ch 101 sts (or any multiple of 8 plus 5 sts).

Row 1 (RS): Beg in the second ch from hook, *1 sc in each of next 4 chs, 1 dc in each of next 4 chs; rep from * across to last 4 chs, 1 sc in each of next 4 chs, turn.

Row 2 (WS): Ch 1 (does not count as st here and throughout), *1 sc in each of next 4 sc, 1 dc in each of next 4 dc; rep from * across to last 4 sc, 1 sc in each of next 4 sc, changing to Color B on final sc, turn.

Row 3: With Color B, ch 3 (counts as dc here and throughout), 1 dc in each of next 3 sc, *1 sc in each of next 4 dc, 1 dc in each of next 4 sc; rep from * to last 4 sc, 1 dc in each of next 4 sc, turn.

Row 4: Ch 3, 1 dc in each of next 3 dc, *1 sc in each of next 4 sc, 1 dc in each of next 4 dc; rep from * across to last 4 dc, 1 dc in each of next 4 dc, changing to Color A on final dc, turn.

Row 5: With Color A, ch 1, *1 sc in each of next 4 dc, 1 dc in each of next 4 sc; rep from * to last 4 dc, 1 dc in each of next 4 sc, turn.

Rep Rows 2–5 another 22 times.

Rep Row 1 once more. Fasten off and cut Color A; Color B will be used for remainder of blanket.

Single Crochet Border

Rnd 1: With Color B, work a single crochet border around the blanket. When working the corners, work 3 sc into corner, then mark the center st of the 3 sc with a locking stitch marker—4 locking stitch markers in total (one in each corner).

Rnd 2: Work another rnd of single crochet, working 3 sc into the marked corner stitches. Fasten off.

Finishing

Weave in ends. Lightly steam and block if desired.

The single crochet border creates a neat, finished edge that will hold up to daily use.

Use the following chart as a general guide for sizing any blanket projects.

BLANKET SIZE GUIDE		
	Lenth	**Width**
Car Seat	48" (121.9cm)	36" (91.4cm)
Receiving	40" (101.6cm)	40" (101.6cm)
Crib	60" (152.4cm)	45" (114.3cm)
Toddler	48" (121.9cm)	42" (106.7cm)
Throw	72" (182.9cm)	60" (152.4cm)
Twin	96" (243.8cm)	66" (167.6cm)
Full/Queen	100" (254cm)	90" (228.6cm)
King	110" (279.4cm)	110" (279.4cm)

About the Author

Jen Lucas has been crocheting for nearly two decades. She has designed hundreds of knitting and crochet patterns for yarn companies, magazines, and books, in addition to her dozens of self-published designs. Jen is the author of seven knitting books, including the bestseller, *Sock-Yarn Shawls*. She lives in Northern Illinois with her husband, Alex, and a home full of crafts. Learn more about Jen at *craftyjencrafts.com*.